S0-ASJ-971

ROMANTIC LOVE

DR. JAMES DOBSON

COUNSELS YOU ON

ROMANTIC LOVE

USING YOUR HEAD IN MATTERS OF THE HEART

Regal Books

A Division of GL Publications
Ventura, California, U.S.A.

Published by Regal Books
A Division of GL Publications
Ventura, California 93006
Printed in U.S.A.

Scripture quotations in this publication are taken from:
The HOLY BIBLE: NEW INTERNATIONAL VERSION. Copyright
© 1973, 1978, 1984 International Bible Society. Used by permission
of Zondervan Bible Publishers.

© Copyright 1989 by Regal Books.
All rights reserved.

Library of Congress Cataloging-in-Publication Data applied for

1 2 3 4 5 6 7 8 9 10 / 91 90 89

Rights for publishing this book in other languages are contracted
by Gospel Literature International (GLINT) foundation. GLINT
also provides technical help for the adaptation, translation, and
publishing of Bible study resources and books in scores of languages worldwide. For further information, contact GLINT, Post
Office Box 488, Rosemead, California, 91770, U.S.A., or the publisher.

This book is affectionately dedicated to my wife Shirley, who believed in me even before I believed in myself. I've shared the greatest moments of my life with this fine lady, and I thank God for bringing her into my life.

CONTENTS

INTRODUCTION

You are about to read a book about one of the strongest and most misunderstood of all human emotions—romantic love. The topic of human emotions always reminds me of a story my mother told about the high school she attended in 1930. It was located in a small Oklahoma town that had produced a series of terrible football teams. Understandably, the students and their parents began to get depressed and dispirited by the drubbing their troops were given every Friday night. It must have been awful.

Finally, a wealthy oil producer decided to take matters in his own hands. He asked to speak to the team in the locker room after yet another devastating defeat. What followed was one of the most dramatic football speeches of all time. This businessman proceeded to offer a brand new Ford to every boy on the team and to each coach if they

Seven days of hoorah and whoop-de-do simply couldn't compensate for the players' lack of discipline and conditioning and practice and study and coaching and drill and experience and character. Such is the nature of romantic love.

would simply defeat their bitter rivals in the next game. Knute Rockne couldn't have said it better.

The team went crazy with sheer delight. They howled and cheered and slapped each other on their padded behinds. At night they dreamed about touchdowns and rumble seats. The entire school caught the spirit of ecstasy, and a holiday fever pervaded the campus. Each player could visualize himself behind the wheel of a gorgeous coupe, with eight gorgeous girls hanging all over his gorgeous body.

Finally, the big night arrived and the team assembled in the locker room. Excitement was at an unprecedented high. The coach made several inane comments and the boys hurried out to face the enemy. They assembled on the sidelines, put their hands together and shouted a simultaneous "Rah!" Then they ran onto the field and were demolished, 38-0.

The team's exuberance did not translate into a single point on the scoreboard. Seven days of hoorah and whoop-de-do simply couldn't compensate for the players' lack of discipline and conditioning and practice and study and coaching and drill and experience and character. Such is the nature of all emotions, particularly romantic love. It has a definite place in human affairs, but when forced to stand alone, it usually reveals itself to be unreliable and ephemeral and even a bit foolish.

While it would be a mistake to minimize the effects of romantic love on our behavior and actions, the important thing to remember is that *emotions—not only romantic love, but all emotions—must always be accountable to the faculties of reason and will.* That accountability is doubly important for those of us who purport to be Christians. If we are to be defeated during life's spiritual pilgrimage, it is likely that negative emotions will play a dominant role in that discouragement. Satan is devastatingly effective in using the weapons of guilt, rejection, fear, embarrassment, grief, depression, loneliness and misunderstanding. Indeed, human beings are vulnerable creatures who could not withstand these satanic pressures without divine assistance.

As we discuss the very powerful emotion of romantic love, we will address the following questions:

1. How can the "feeling of love" become a dangerous trap?
2. Why do so many couples become disillusioned shortly after the honeymoon?
3. Does "love at first sight" ever occur?
4. Does God select one particular person for us to marry and then guide us together?
5. How can love be kept alive?

Following our discussion on romantic love is a section called "Learning-Discussion Ideas." The objective is to permit the material to be used in Sunday School classes, neighborhood Bible study classes, or any other setting where it might be beneficial. Since virtually every human being has dealt with this common emotion at some point, it is often helpful to share experiences with sympathetic friends and fellow Christians. In other instances, individuals will be able to use the reference pages personally.

Finally, we will touch on the "Interpretation of Impressions" in regard to guidance in dealing with the emotion of romantic love, in order that we might benefit from God's gift of love to man, rather than be destroyed by Satan's counterfeit of that gift.

ROMANTIC LOVE: DISTORTION VERSUS THE REAL THING

It has been of concern to me that many young people grow up with a very distorted concept of romantic love. They are taught to confuse the real thing with infatuation and to idealize marriage into something it can never be. To help remedy this situation, I developed a brief true or false quiz for use in teaching groups of teenagers. But to my surprise, I found that adults did not score much higher on the quiz than their adolescent offspring.

You may want to take this quiz to measure your understanding of romance, love and marriage. A discussion of each true-false statement follows the quiz to help you discover for yourself the difference between distorted love and the real thing.

What Do You Believe About Love?
Please check the appropriate column.

		True	False
Item	1: "Love at first sight" occurs between some people.	☐	☐
Item	2: It is easy to distinguish real love from infatuation.	☐	☐
Item	3: People who sincerely love each other will not fight and argue.	☐	☐
Item	4: God selects *one* particular person for each of us to marry, and He will guide us together.	☐	☐
Item	5: If a man and woman genuinely love each other, then hardships and troubles will have little or no effect on their relationship.	☐	☐
Item	6: It is better to marry the wrong person than to remain single and lonely throughout life.	☐	☐

The confusion begins when boy meets girl and the entire sky lights up in romantic profusion. Smoke and fire are followed by lightning and thunder, and alas, the starry-eyed couple find themselves knee-deep in true love.

Item   7: It is not harmful to have   ☐   ☐
          sexual intercourse
          before marriage if the
          couple has a meaningful
          relationship.

Item   8: If a couple is genuinely   ☐   ☐
          in love, that condition is
          permanent—lasting a
          lifetime.

Item   9: Short courtships (six   ☐   ☐
          months or less) are
          best.

Item 10: Teenagers are more   ☐   ☐
          capable of genuine love
          than are older people.

Boy Meets Girl—Hooray for Love!

While there are undoubtedly some differences of
opinion regarding the answers for the true-false
quiz, I feel strongly about what I consider to be
correct responses to each item. In fact, I believe
many of the common marital hang-ups develop
from a misunderstanding of these 10 issues.

Let's look at a hypothetical courtship where
the meaning of love is poorly understood.

The confusion begins when boy meets girl and
the entire sky lights up in romantic profusion.
Smoke and fire are followed by lightning and thun-

der, and alas, the starry-eyed couple find themselves knee-deep in true love. Adrenalin is pumped into the cardiovascular system by the pint, and every nerve is charged with 110 volts of electricity. Then two little fellows go racing up the respective backbones and blast their exhilarated messages into each spinning head: "This is it! The search is over! You've found the perfect human being! Hooray for love!"

For our romantic young couple, it is simply too wonderful to behold. They want to be together 24 hours a day—to take walks in the rain and sit by the fire and kiss and smooch and cuddle. They get all choked up just thinking about each other. And it doesn't take long for the subject of marriage to propose itself. So they set the date and reserve the chapel and contact the minister and order the flowers.

The big night arrives amidst Mother's tears and Dad's grins and jealous bridesmaids and frightened little flower girls. The candles are lit and two beautiful songs are butchered by the bride's sister. Then the vows are muttered, rings placed on trembling fingers, and the preacher tells the groom to kiss his new wife. Then they sprint up the aisle, each flashing 32 teeth, on the way to the reception room.

Their friends and well-wishers hug and kiss the bride and roll their eyes at the groom, eat the

awful cake, and follow the instructions of the per-
spiring photographer. Finally the new Mr. and
Mrs. run from the church in a flurry of rice and
confetti and strike out on their honeymoon. So far
the beautiful dream remains intact, but it is living
on borrowed time.

The first night in the motel is not only less
exciting than advertised—it turns into a comical
disaster. She is exhausted and tense, and he is
self-conscious and phony. From the beginning, sex
is tinged with the threat of possible failure. Their
vast expectations about the marital bed lead to disappointment and frustration and fear. Since most
human beings have an almost neurotic desire to
feel sexually adequate, each partner tends to
blame his mate for their orgasmic problems, which
eventually adds a note of anger and resentment to
their relationship.

About three o'clock on the second afternoon,
the new husband gives 10 minutes thought to the
fateful question, "Have I made an enormous mistake?" His silence increases her anxieties, and the
seeds of disenchantment are born. Each partner
has far too much time to think about the consequences of this new relationship, and they both
begin to feel trapped.

Their initial argument is a silly thing. They
struggle momentarily over how much money to
spend for dinner on the third night of the honey-

moon. She wants to go someplace romantic to charge up the atmosphere, and he wants to eat with Ronald McDonald. The flare-up lasts only a few moments and is followed by apologies, but some harsh words have been exchanged, which took the keen edge off the beautiful dream. They will soon learn to hurt each other more effectively.

Somehow, they make it through the six-day trip and drive home to set up housekeeping together. Then the world starts to splinter and disintegrate before their eyes. The next fight is bigger and better than the first; he leaves home for two hours and she calls her mother.

Throughout the first year, they will be engaged in an enormous contest of wills, each vying for power and leadership. And in the midst of this tug-of-war, she staggers out of the obstetrician's office with the words ringing in her ears, "I have some good news for you, Mrs. Jones!" If there is anything on earth Mrs. Jones doesn't need at that time, it is "good news" from an obstetrician.

From there to the final conflict, we see two disappointed, confused and deeply hurt young people, wondering how it all came about. We also see a little tow-headed lad who will never enjoy the benefits of a stable home. He'll be raised by his mother and will always wonder, "Why doesn't Dad live here anymore?"

The picture I have painted does not reflect every young marriage, obviously, but it is representative of far too many of them. The divorce rate is higher in America than in any other civilized nation in the world, and it is rising. In the case of our disillusioned young couple, what happened to their romantic dream? How did the relationship that began with such enthusiasm turn so quickly into hatred and hostility? They could not possibly have been more enamored with each other at the beginning, but their "happiness" blew up in their startled faces. Why didn't it last? How can others avoid the same unpleasant surprise?

First we need to understand the true meaning of romantic love. Perhaps the answers to our quiz will help accomplish that objective.

BELIEFS ABOUT LOVE

Item 1: "Love at first sight" occurs between some people—true or false?

Though some readers will disagree with me, love at first sight is a physical and emotional impossibility. Why? Because love is not simply a feeling of romantic excitement; it goes beyond intense sexual attraction; it exceeds the thrill at having "captured" a highly desirable social prize. These are emotions that are unleashed at first sight, but they *do not constitute love.* I wish the whole world knew that fact. These temporary feelings differ from love in that they place the spotlight on the one experiencing them. "What is happening to *Me*? This is the most fantastic thing *I've* ever been through! *I* think I am in love!"

You see, these emotions are selfish in the sense that they are motivated by our own gratification. They have little to do with the new lover.

Such a person has not fallen in love with another person; *he has fallen in love with love!* And there is an enormous difference between the two.

The popular songs in the world of teenage music reveal a vast ignorance of the meaning of love. One immortal number asserts, "Before the dance was through, I knew I was in luv with yew." I wonder if the crooner will be quite so confident tomorrow morning. Another confesses, "I didn't know just what to do, so I whispered "I luv yew!"" That one really gets to me. The idea of basing a lifetime commitment on sheer confusion seems a bit shaky, at best.

The Partridge Family recorded a song which also betrays a lack of understanding of real love; it said, "I woke up in love today 'cause I went to sleep with you on my mind." You see, love in this sense is nothing more than a frame of mind—it's just about that permanent. Finally, a rock group of the 60s called *The Doors* takes the prize for the most ignorant musical number of the century; it was called, "Hello, I love you, won't you tell me your name!"

Did you know that the idea of marriage based on romantic affection is a very recent development in human affairs? Prior to A.D. 1200, weddings were arranged by the families of the bride and groom, and it never occurred to anyone that they were supposed to "fall in love." In fact, the concept of romantic love was actually popularized by William Shakespeare. There are times when I wish the old Englishman was here to help us straighten out the mess that he initiated.

Real love, in contrast to popular notions, is an expression of the deepest appreciation for another human being; it is an intense awareness of his or her needs and longings for the past, present and future. It is unselfish and giving and caring. And believe me, these are not attitudes one "falls" into at first sight, as though he were tumbling into a ditch.

I have developed a lifelong love for my wife, but it was not something I fell into. I *grew* into it, and that process took time. I had to know her before I could appreciate the depth and stability of her character—to become acquainted with the nuances of her personality, which I now cherish. The familiarity from which love has blossomed simply could not be generated on "Some enchanted evening . . . across a crowded room." One cannot love an unknown object, regardless of how attractive or sexy or nubile it is!

Item 2: It is easy to distinguish real love from infatuation—true or false?

The answer is, again, false. That wild ride at the start of a romantic adventure bears all the ear-marks of a lifetime trip. Just try to tell a starry-

How many vulnerable young couples "fall in love with love" on the first date—and lock themselves into marriage before the natural swing of their emotions has even progressed through the first dip?

eyed 16-year-old dreamer that he is not really in love—that he's merely infatuated. He'll whip out his guitar and sing you a song about "true love." He knows what he feels, and he feels great. But he'd better enjoy the roller-coaster ride while it lasts, because it has a predictable end point.

I must stress this fact with the greatest emphasis: The exhilaration of infatuation is *never* a permanent condition. Period! If you expect to live on the top of that mountain, year after year, you can forget it! Emotions swing from high to low to high in cyclical rhythm, and since romantic excitement is an emotion, it too will certainly oscillate. If the thrill of sexual encounter is identified as genuine love, then disillusionment and disappointment are already knocking at the door.

How many vulnerable young couples "fall in love with love" on the first date—and lock themselves into marriage before the natural swing of their emotions has even progressed through the first dip? They then wake up one morning without that neat feeling and conclude that love has died. In reality, it was never there in the first place. They were fooled by an emotional "high."

I was trying to explain this up-and-down characteristic of our psychological nature to a group of 100 young married couples to whom I was speaking. During the discussion period, someone asked a young man in the group why he got married so young, and he replied, "'Cause I didn't know 'bout that wiggly line until it was too late!" Alas, 'tis true. That wiggly line has trapped more than one young romanticist.

The "wiggly line" is manipulated up and down by the circumstances of life. Even when a man and woman love each other deeply and genuinely, they will find themselves supercharged on one occasion and emotionally bland on another. You see, their love is not defined by the highs and lows, but is dependent *on a commitment of their will.* Stability comes from this irrepressible determination to make a success of marriage and to keep the flame aglow *regardless of the circumstances.*

Unfortunately, not everyone agrees with the divinely inspired concept of permanent marriage. We have heard the noted anthropologist Dr. Margaret Mead advocate trial marriage for the young; we have been propagandized to accept communal marriage and contract marriage and cohabitation. Even our music has reflected our aimless groping for an innovative relationship between men and women.

One such idea is that romantic love can only survive in the *absence* of permanent commitment. Singer Glen Campbell translated this thought into music in his once popular song entitled "Gentle on My Mind." Paraphrasing the lyrics, he said it was not the ink-stained signatures dried on some marriage certificate that kept his bedroll stashed behind the couch in his lover's home; it was knowing that he could get up and leave her anytime he wished—that she had no hooks into his hide. It was the freedom to abandon her that kept her "gentle on [his] mind."

What a ridiculous notion to think a woman exists who could let her lover come and go with no feelings of loss, rejection, or abandonment. How ignorant it is of the power of love (and sex) to make us "one flesh," inevitably ripping and tearing that flesh at the time of separation.

And, of course, Brother Campbell's song said nothing about the little children who are born from such a relationship, each one wondering if Daddy will be there tomorrow morning, if he will help them pay their bills, or if he'll be out by a railroad track somewhere sipping coffee from a tin can and thinking the good thoughts in the backroads of his mind. Can't you see his little woman standing with her children in the front doorway, waving a hanky and calling, "Good-bye, Dear. Drop in when you can"?

Let's return to the question before us: if genuine love is rooted in a commitment of the will, how can one know when it arrives? How can it be distinguished from temporary infatuation? How can the feeling be interpreted if it is unreliable and inconstant?

The best advice I can give a couple contemplating marriage is this: make no important, life-shaping decisions quickly or impulsively, and when in doubt, stall for time.

There is only one answer to those questions: *it takes time.* The best advice I can give a couple contemplating marriage (or any other important decision) is this: make *no* important, life-shaping decisions quickly or impulsively, and when in doubt, stall for time. That's not a bad suggestion for all of us to apply.

Item 3: People who sincerely love each other will not fight and argue—true or false?

I doubt if this third item actually requires an answer. Some marital conflict is as inevitable as the sunrise, even in loving marriages. There is a difference, however, between healthy and unhealthy combat, depending on the way the disagreement is handled. In an unstable marriage, anger is usually hurled directly at the partner. Hostile, person-centered "you messages" strike at the heart of one's self-worth and produce intensive internal upheaval:

"You never do anything right!"

"Why did I ever marry you?"

"How can you be so stupid (or unreasonable or unfair)?"

"You are getting more like your mother every day."

The wounded partner often responds in like manner, hurling back every unkind and hateful remark he or she can concoct, punctuated with tears and profanity. The avowed purpose of this kind of in-fighting is to hurt, and it does. The cutting words will never be forgotten, even though uttered in a moment of irrational anger. Such combat is not only unhealthy; it is vicious and corrosive. It erodes the marriage relationship, and can easily destroy it.

Healthy conflict, on the other hand, remains focused on the issue around which the disagreement began. Issue-centered "I" messages let your partner know what is wrong, but that he or she is not the main target:

"I'm worried about all these bills."

"I get upset when I don't know you'll be late for dinner."

"I was embarrassed by what you said at the party last night—I felt foolish."

Any area of struggle—worry, anger, embarrassment—can be emotional and tense, but it can be much less damaging to the egos of both spouses if they will focus on the basic disagreement and try to resolve it together. A healthy couple can work through problems by compromise and negotiation. There will still be pain and hurt, but a husband and wife will have fewer imbedded barbs to pluck out the following morning.

The ability to fight *properly* may be the most important concept to be learned by newlyweds.

Those who never comprehend the technique are usually left with two alternatives: (1) turn the anger and resentment inward in silence, where it will fester and accumulate through the years, or (2) blast away at the personhood of one's mate. The divorce courts are well represented by couples in both categories.[1]

Item 4: God selects one particular person for each of us to marry, and He will guide us together— true or false?

A young man whom I was counseling once told me that he awoke in the middle of the night with the strong impression that God wanted him to marry a young lady whom he had dated casually only a few times. They were not even going together at that moment and hardly knew each other. The next morning he called her and relayed the message that God had supposedly sent him during the night. The girl figured she shouldn't argue with God, and she accepted the proposal. They have now been married for seven years and have struggled for survival since their wedding day!

Anyone who believes that God guarantees a successful marriage to every Christian is in for a shock. This is not to say that He is disinterested in the choice of a mate, or that He will not answer a specific request for guidance on this all-important decision. Certainly, His will should be sought in such a critical matter, and I consulted Him repeatedly before proposing to my wife.

However, I do not believe that God performs a routine matchmaking service for everyone who worships Him. He has given us judgment, common sense and discretionary powers, and He expects us to exercise these abilities in matters matrimonial. Those who believe otherwise are likely to enter marriage glibly, thinking, "God would have stopped us if He didn't approve." To such confident people I can only say, "Lotsa luck."

Item 5: If a man and woman genuinely love each other, then hardships and troubles will have little or no effect on their relationship—true or false?
Another common misconception about the meaning of "true love" is that it inevitably stands like the rock of Gibraltar against the storms of life. Many people apparently believe that love is destined to conquer all. The Beatles endorsed this notion with their song, "All we need is love, love, love is all we need." Unfortunately, we need a bit more.

As I mentioned before, I have served on the Attending Staff for Children's Hospital of Los Angeles. We have seen numerous genetic and metabolic problems throughout the years, most of which involved mental retardation in our young patients. The emotional impact of such a diagnosis on the families is sometimes devastating. Even in stable, loving marriages, the guilt and disappointment of having produced a "broken" child often drives a wedge of isolation between the distressed mother and father. In a similar manner, the fiber of love can be weakened by financial hardships, disease, business setbacks or prolonged separation. In short, we must conclude that love is vulnerable to pain and trauma, and often wobbles when assaulted by life.

Item 6: It is better to marry the wrong person than to remain single and lonely throughout life—true or false?

Again, the answer is false. Generally speaking, it is less painful to be searching for an end to loneliness than to be embroiled in the emotional combat of a sour marriage. Yet the threat of being an "old maid" (a term I detest) causes many girls to grab the first train that rambles down the marital track. And, too often, it offers a one-way ticket to disaster.

The fear of never finding a mate can cause a single person to ignore his better judgment and compromise his own standards. A young woman, particularly, may argue with herself in this manner: "John isn't a Christian, but maybe I can influence him after we're married. He drinks too much, but that's probably because he's young and

When one plunges into marriage despite the obvious warning flags, he is gambling with the remaining years of his earthly existence.

carefree. And we don't have much in common, but I'm sure we'll learn to love each other more as time passes. Besides, what could be worse than living alone?"

This kind of rationalization is based on a desperate hope for a matrimonial miracle, but storybook endings are uncommon events in everyday life. When one plunges into marriage despite the obvious warning flags, he is gambling with the remaining years of his earthly existence.

For those readers who are single today, *please* believe me when I say that a bad marriage is among the most miserable experiences on earth! It is filled with rejection and hurt feelings and hatred and screaming and broken children and sleepless nights. Certainly, a solitary walk as a single person can be a meaningful and fulfilling life; at least, it does not involve "a house divided against itself."

Item 7: It is not harmful to have sexual intercourse before marriage, if the couple has a meaningful relationship—true or false?

This item represents *the* most dangerous of the popular misconceptions about romantic love, not only for individuals but for our future as a nation. During the past several years we have witnessed the tragic disintegration of our sexual mores and traditional concepts of morality. Responding to a steady onslaught by the entertainment industry and by the media, our people have begun to believe that premarital intercourse is a noble experience, extramarital encounters are healthy, homosexuality is acceptable, and bisexuality is even better. These views—labeled as "the new morality"—reflect the sexual stupidity of the age in which we live, yet they are believed and applied by millions of American citizens.

A recent study of college students revealed that 25 percent of them have shared bedrooms with a member of the opposite sex for at least three months. According to *Life Styles and Campus Communities,* 66 percent of college students reportedly believe premarital intercourse is acceptable between any two people who consent or "when a couple has dated some and care a lot about each other."

I have never considered myself to be a prophet of doom, but I am admittedly alarmed by statistical evidence of this nature. I view these trends with fear and trepidation, seeing in them the potential death of our society and our way of life.

Mankind has known intuitively for at least 50 centuries that indiscriminate sexual activity represents both an individual and a corporate threat to survival. And history bears it out. Anthropologist J.D. Unwin conducted an exhaustive study of the

88 civilizations that have existed in the history of the world. Each culture has reflected a similar life cycle, beginning with a strict code of sexual conduct and ending with the demand for complete "freedom" to express individual passion. Unwin reports that *every* society that extended sexual permissiveness to its people was soon to perish. There have been no exceptions. [2]

Why do you suppose the reproductive urge within us is so relevant to cultural survival? It is because the energy that holds a people together is sexual in nature! The physical attraction between men and women causes them to establish a family and invest themselves in its development. It encourages them to work and save and toil to insure the survival of their families. Their sexual energy provides the impetus for the raising of healthy children and for the transfer of values from one generation to the next.

Sexual drives urge a man to work when he would rather play. They cause a woman to save when she would rather spend. In short, the sexual aspect of our nature—when released exclusively within the family—produces stability and responsibility that would not otherwise occur. When a nation is composed of millions of devoted, responsible family units, the entire society is stable, responsible and resilient.

If sexual energy within the family is the key to

a healthy society, then its release outside those boundaries is potentially catastrophic. The very force that binds a people together then becomes the agent for its own destruction.

Perhaps this point can be illustrated by an analogy between sexual energy in the nuclear family and physical energy in the nucleus of a tiny atom. Electrons, neutrons and protons are held in delicate balance by an electrical force within each atom. But when that atom and its neighbors are split in nuclear fission (such as in an atomic bomb), the energy that had provided the internal stability is then released with unbelievable power and destruction. There is ample reason to believe that this comparison between the atom and the family is more than incidental.

Who can deny that a society is seriously weakened when the intense sexual urge between men and women becomes an instrument for suspicion and intrigue within millions of individual families:

- when a woman never knows what her husband is doing when away from home;

- when a husband can't trust his wife in his absence;

- when half of the brides are pregnant at the altar;

- when both newlyweds have slept with numer-

Illegitimate births, heartbreak, shattered personalities, abortions, disease, even death—this is the true vomitus of the sexual revolution, and I am tired of hearing it romanticized and glorified.

ous partners, losing the exclusive wonder of the marital bed;

- when everyone is doing his own thing, particularly that which brings him immediate sensual gratification!

Unfortunately, the most devastated victim of an immoral society of this nature is the vulnerable child who hears his parents scream and argue. Their tensions and frustrations spill over into his world, and the instability of his home leaves its ugly scars on his young mind. Then he watches his parents separate in anger, and he says good-bye to the father he needs and loves.

Or perhaps we should speak of the thousands of babies born to unmarried teenage mothers each year—many of whom will never know the meaning of a warm, nurturing home. Or maybe we should discuss the rampant scourge of venereal disease, including the deadly AIDS virus, which has reached epidemic proportions.

Illegitimate births, heartbreak, shattered personalities, abortions, disease, even death—this is the true vomitus of the sexual revolution, and I am tired of hearing it romanticized and glorified. God has clearly forbidden irresponsible sexual behavior, not to deprive us of fun and pleasure, but to spare us the disastrous consequences of this festering way of life. Those individuals and those nations choosing to defy His commandments on this issue will pay a dear price for their folly.

Item 8: If a couple is genuinely in love, that condition is permanent—lasting a lifetime—true or false?
Love, even genuine love, is a fragile thing. It must be maintained and protected if it is to survive. Love can perish when a husband or wife works seven days a week, when there is no time for romantic activity, when the man and woman forget how to talk to each other.

The keen edge in a loving relationship may be dulled through the routine pressures of living, as I experienced during the early days of my marriage to Shirley. I was working full time and trying to finish my doctorate at the University of Southern California. My wife was teaching school and maintaining our small home. I remember clearly the evening that I realized what this busy life was doing to our relationship. We still loved each other, but it had been too long since we had felt a spirit of warmth and closeness. My textbooks were pushed aside that night and we went for a long walk. The following semester I carried a very light load in school and postponed my academic goals so as to preserve that which I valued more highly.

Where does your marriage rank on your hierarchy of values? Does it get the leftovers and scraps from your busy schedule or is it something

Adolescent romance is an exciting part of growing up, but it seldom meets the criteria for the deeper relationships of which successful marriages are composed.

of great worth to be preserved and supported? It can die if left untended.

Item 9: Short courtships (six months or less) are best—true or false?

The answer to this question is incorporated in the reply to the second item regarding infatuation. Short courtships require impulsive decisions about lifetime commitments, and that is risky business, at best.

Item 10: Teenagers are more capable of genuine love than are older people—true or false?

If this item were true, then we would be hard pressed to explain why approximately half the teenage marriages end in divorce in the first few years. To the contrary, the kind of love I have been describing—unselfish, giving, caring commitment—requires a sizeable dose of maturity to make it work. And maturity is a partial thing in most teenagers. Adolescent romance is an exciting part of growing up, but it seldom meets the criteria for the deeper relationships of which successful marriages are composed.

Notes
1. For more information on how to handle conflict in a healthy way, read David Augsburger, *Caring Enough to Confront,* rev. ed. (Ventura, CA: Regal Books, 1980).
2. J.D. Unwin, *Sexual Regulations and Cultural Behavior.* Copyright 1969 by Frank M. Darrow, P.O. Box 305, Trona, California 93562.

I AM COMMITTED TO YOU

All 10 items on this brief questionnaire are false, for they represent the 10 most common misconceptions about the meaning of romantic love. Sometimes I wish the test could be used as a basis for issuing marriage licenses: those scoring 9 or 10 would qualify with honor; those getting 5-8 items right would be required to wait an extra 6 months before marriage; those confused dreamers answering 4 or less items correctly would be recommended for permanent celibacy! (Seriously, what we probably need is a cram-course for everyone contemplating wedding bells.)

In conclusion, I want to share the words I wrote to my wife on an anniversary card on our eighth anniversary. What I said to her may not be expressed in the way you would communicate with your mate. I do hope, however, that my words illustrate the "genuine, uncompromising love" I have been describing:

> *To My Darlin' Little Wife, Shirley*
> *on the occasion of our Eighth Anniversary*
>
> *I'm sure you remember the many, many occasions during our eight years of marriage when the tide of love and affection soared high above the crest—times when our feeling for each other was almost limitless. This kind of intense emotion can't be brought about voluntarily, but it often accompanies a time of particular happiness. We felt it when I was offered my first professional position. We felt it when the world's most precious child came home from the maternity ward of Huntington Hospital. We felt it when the University of California chose to award a doctoral degree to me. But emotions are strange! We felt the same closeness when the opposite kind of event took place; when threat and potential disaster entered our lives. We felt an intense closeness when a medical problem threatened to postpone our marriage plans. We felt it when you were hospitalized last year. I felt it intensely when I knelt over your unconscious form after a grinding automobile accident.*

I'm trying to say this: both happiness and threat bring that overwhelming appreciation and affection for a person's beloved sweetheart. But the fact is, most of life is made up of neither disaster nor unusual hilarity. Rather, it is composed of the routine, calm, everyday events in which we participate. And during these times, I enjoy the quiet, serene love that actually surpasses the effervescent display, in many ways. It is not as exuberant, perhaps, but it runs deep and solid. I find myself firmly in that kind of love on this Eighth Anniversary. Today I feel the steady and quiet affection that comes from a devoted heart. I am committed to you and your happiness, now more than I've ever been. I want to remain your "sweetheart."

When events throw us together emotionally, we will enjoy the thrill and romantic excitement. But during life's routine, like today, my love stands undiminished. Happy Anniversary to my wonderful wife.

Jim

The key phrase in my note to Shirley is, "I am committed to you." My love for my wife is not blown back and forth by the winds of change, by

I love you as long as I feel attracted to you—or as long as someone else doesn't look better—or as long as it is to my advantage to continue the relationship. Sooner or later, this unanchored love will certainly vaporize.

circumstances and environmental influences. Even though my fickle emotions jump from one extreme to another, my commitment remains solidly anchored. I have chosen to love my wife, and that choice is sustained by an uncompromising will.

The essential investment of commitment is sorely missing in so many modern marriages. I love you, they seem to say, as long as I feel attracted to you—or as long as someone else doesn't look better—or as long as it is to my advantage to continue the relationship. Sooner or later, this unanchored love will certainly vaporize.

"For better or worse, for richer, for poorer, in sickness and in health, to love and to cherish, till death us do part . . . . "

That familiar pledge from the past still offers the most solid foundation upon which to build a marriage, for therein lies the real meaning of genuine romantic love.

LEARNING-
DISCUSSION IDEAS

Are you reading this book alone? With your
spouse? With a study group? Whatever your situation, the following questions, agree/disagree
statements, life-situations and Bible study ideas
will help you work with Dr. Dobson's views as he
discusses 10 common misconceptions about
romance, love, marriage. Equip yourself with a
notebook, Bible and pencil and you are ready to
work with these learning-discussion ideas.

**Item 1: "Love at first sight" occurs between some
people—true or false?**

1. Do you agree or disagree with Dr. Dobson's view that "love at first sight" is physically
and emotionally impossible? Can the kind of rela-

tionship described in Philippians exist in "love at first sight"? Why? Why Not?

Then make my joy complete by being like-minded, having the same love, being one in spirit and purpose (Phil. 2:2).

2. Do you agree with Dr. Dobson that popular songs help distort a person's concept of love? What about films? TV? Magazine fiction? How can you tell the difference between "falling in love with love" and developing a genuine love relationship with someone? What does a passage like Colossians 3:12-15 have to do with "true love" in a marriage?

Therefore, as God's chosen people, holy and dearly loved, clothe yourselves with compassion, kindness, humility, gentleness and patience. Bear with each other and forgive whatever grievances you may have against one another. Forgive as the Lord forgave you. And over all these virtues put on love, which binds them all together in perfect unity. Let the peace of Christ rule in your hearts, since as members of one body you were called to peace.

3. Is selfishness involved in "love at first sight"? Why? Why not? For ideas on love and selfishness read Philippians 2:2-4.

Then make my joy complete by being like-

minded, having the same love, being one in spirit and purpose. Do nothing out of selfish ambition or vain conceit, but in humility consider others better than yourselves. Each of you should look not only to your own interests, but also to the interests of others.

4. Read the last two paragraphs in Dr. Dobson's discussion of "love at first sight" (p. 25, paragraph beginning, "Real love . . . "). List reasons the words "time" and "grow" are important to real love. Read the following as well as other versions of 1 Corinthians 13:4-7 and note words and phrases that you feel are related to the idea of taking time to grow into love.

Love is patient, love is kind. It does not envy, it does not boast, it is not proud. It is not rude, it is not self-seeking, it is not easily angered, it keeps no record of wrongs. Love does not delight in evil but rejoices with the truth. It always protects, always trusts, always hopes, always perseveres.

Item 2: It is easy to distinguish real love from infatuation—true or false?

1. Do you agree or disagree with Dr. Dobson that: "The exhilaration of infatuation is *never* a permanent condition"?

Discussion ideas: Is any relationship immune from ups and downs? Is any situation permanent?

Can anyone truthfully say, "I won't change"? Read the following Scripture:

"I the Lord do not change. So you, O descendants of Jacob, are not destroyed" (Mal. 3:6).

Jesus Christ is the same yesterday and today and forever (Heb. 13:8).

How can God's changelessness strengthen and give stability to a human relationship? *But the plans of the Lord stand firm forever, the purposes of his heart through all generations* (Ps. 33:11).

2. Does the following statement by Dr. Dobson strike you as (1) unromantic; (2) puzzling; (3) false; (4) a solid base for marriage? "Stability [in marriage] comes from this irrepressible determination to make a success of marriage, and to keep the flame aglow *regardless of the circumstances.*" Explain your response. How do the following verses compare with that statement?

May the God who gives endurance and encouragement give you a spirit of unity among yourselves as you follow Christ Jesus (Rom. 15:5).

Therefore encourage one another and build each other up, just as in fact you are doing (1 Thess. 5:11).

3. According to Dr. Dobson what is the necessary ingredient that must be added before you can

really determine whether a person is experiencing infatuation or genuine love? Proverbs 19:2 talks about the wisdom of taking time to think through any important step when it says: *It is not good to have zeal without knowledge, nor to be hasty and miss the way.* How can this apply to evaluating infatuation and real love? What are the unknowns?

Item 3: People who sincerely love each other will not fight and argue—true or false?

1. "Some marital conflict is inevitable," says Dr. Dobson. What is the key to keeping the combat zone healthy? Read Dr. Dobson's comments in the two paragraphs following Item 3. For additional ideas read the verses listed below:

A gentle answer turns away wrath, but a harsh word stirs up anger . . . . A hot-tempered man stirs up dissension, but a patient man calms a quarrel (Prov. 15:1,18).

Starting a quarrel is like breaching a dam; so drop the matter before a dispute breaks out (Prov. 17:14).

"In your anger do not sin": Do not let the sun go down while you are still angry, and do not give the evil a foothold (Eph. 4:26,27).

2. True or false? Can a married couple argue and still obey the teaching in Ephesians 4:31? *Get*

rid of all bitterness, rage and anger, brawling and slander, along with every form of malice.

3. Discuss the difference between being angry at your spouse and being angry or hurt by the issue or the problem. Is it always possible to keep the two separated? What guides for constructive conflict can you find in the following Scripture?

If you keep on biting and devouring each other, watch out or you will be destroyed by each other (Gal. 5:15).

Above all, love each other deeply, because love covers over a multitude of sins (1 Pet. 4:8).

Therefore confess your sins to each other and pray for each other so that you may be healed. The prayer of a righteous man is powerful and effective (Jas. 5:16).

Read the verses in as many versions as possible. List three key ideas.

4. If you are in a study group situation, ask volunteers to role-play an argument that demonstrates the principle: "healthy conflict . . . remains focused on the issue around which the disagreement began." For each role-play choose from the following three issues:

"I'm worried about all these bills."

"I get upset when I don't know you'll be late for dinner."

"I was embarrassed by what you said at the party last night—I felt foolish."

After each role-play argument take a few minutes for the entire group to evaluate: did the argument stay on the issue, or did it become personal?

Item 4: God selects one particular person for each of us to marry and He will guide us together— true or false?

1. How does God offer help for choosing a marriage partner? Before you decide on your answer read the following Scripture:

"Call to me and I will answer you and tell you great and unsearchable things you do not know" (Jer. 33:3).

Look to the Lord and his strength; seek his face always (1 Chron. 16:11).

Do not be anxious about anything, but in everything, by prayer and petition, with thanksgiving, present your requests to God (Phil. 4:6).

If any of you lacks wisdom, he should ask God, who gives generously to all without finding fault, and it will be given to him. But when he asks, he must believe and not doubt, because he who doubts is like a wave of the sea, blown and tossed by the wind. That man should not think he will receive anything from the Lord; he is a double-minded man, unstable in all he does (Jas. 1:5-8).

Is the help described in these verses general or specific?

2. What does the Bible reveal about God's will for a Christian's choice of a marriage partner?

Do not be yoked together with unbelievers. For what do righteousness and wickedness have in common? Or what fellowship can light have with darkness? (2 Cor. 6:14).

In your opinion, what is more important: that a prospective mate be a Christian or that he or she be mature, kind, patient, etc.? Give reasons for your answer.

3. Dr. Dobson says, "Anyone who believes that God guarantees a successful marriage to every Christian is in for a shock." What do you feel he means by this statement? Do you agree or disagree?

Item 5: If a man and woman genuinely love each other, then hardships and troubles will have little or no effect on their relationship—true or false?

1. Do you agree or disagree with Dr. Dobson's belief that the emotional impact of trouble

can be devastating even in a stable, loving marriage? Why? Give real-life evidence (which you have observed) to support your view.

2. What resources do Christian couples have to help them face trouble and work out problems? Which of the following Bible passages would give you the most encouragement in times of trouble?

Have I not commanded you? Be strong and courageous. Do not be terrified; do not be discouraged, for the Lord your God will be with you wherever you go (Josh. 1:9).

From the Lord comes deliverance. May your blessing be on your people (Ps. 3:4).

So then, just as you received Christ Jesus as Lord, continue to live in him, rooted and built up in him, strengthened in the faith as you were taught, and overflowing with thankfulness (Col. 2:6,7).

Be self-controlled and alert. Your enemy the devil prowls around like a roaring lion looking for someone to devour. Resist him, standing firm in the faith, because you know that your brothers throughout the world are undergoing the same kind of sufferings. And the God of all grace, who called you to his eternal glory in Christ, after you have suffered a little while, will himself restore you and make you strong, firm and steadfast. To him be the power for ever and ever. Amen (1 Pet. 5:8-11).

3. Dr. Dobson speaks of the "wedge of isolation" that trouble can drive between a distressed husband and wife (mother and father). Identify at least three principles given in the following Scripture that can help marriage partners reach out to each other in troubled times and avoid the "wedge of isolation."

Dear children, let us not love with words or tongue but with actions and in truth (1 John 3:18).

Dear friends, let us love one another, for love comes from God. Everyone who loves has been born of God and knows God (1 John 4:7).

Therefore encourage one another and build each other up, just as in fact you are doing (1 Thess. 5:11).

Each of you should look not only to your own interests, but also to the interests of others (Phil. 2:4).

4. List ways to protect love from "the pain and trauma" of trouble. From the following Scripture portions, choose ways to protect and strengthen love, even when things are rough:

Carry each other's burdens, and in this way you will fulfill the law of Christ (Gal. 6:2).

Rejoice with those who rejoice; mourn with those who mourn (Rom. 12:15).

Finally, all of you, live in harmony with one

another; be sympathetic, love as brothers, be compassionate and humble. Do not repay evil with evil or insult with insult, but with blessing, because to this you were called so that you may inherit a blessing (1 Pet. 3:8,9).

Which of these ways do you need to work on in your marriage? Which will require the most change in you?

Item 6: It is better to marry the wrong person than to remain single and lonely throughout life— true or false?

1. Dr. Dobson says, "It is [usually] less painful to be searching for an end to loneliness than to be embroiled in the emotional combat of a sour marriage." Do you agree or disagree? Why?

2. Do statements made in the following references favor loneliness or marriage to a "wrong person"?

Better a meal of vegetables where there is love than a fattened calf with hatred (Prov. 15:17).

Better a dry crust with peace and quiet than a house full of feasting, with strife (Prov. 17:1).

Better one handful with tranquillity than two handfuls with toil and chasing after the wind (Eccl. 4:6).

3. List five constructive suggestions for ways a man can combat loneliness. Also list five specific ways a lonely woman can fill her life with meaningful activities. List your ideas under such headings as: Personal Enrichment; Caring About Others; Discovering New Things; Spiritual Growth.

4. In 1 Corinthians 7:8,9 the apostle Paul encourages Christians to remain single, if possible. *Now to the unmarried and the widows I say: It is good for them to stay unmarried, as I am. But if they cannot control themselves, they should marry, for it is better to marry than to burn with passion.* What are some spiritual advantages unmarried people enjoy?

Item 7: It is not harmful to have sexual intercourse before marriage if the couple has a meaningful relationship—true or false?

1. Discuss specific ways the entertainment industry and other media communicate the view that premarital intercourse is acceptable between any two people who consent.

2. Dr. Dobson cites anthropological studies showing how all civilizations that move from a strict code for sexual conduct to wide open "sexual freedom" end in disaster.

How can a society enforce a strict code of sexual conduct and still preserve the freedom of the individual?

3. Dr. Dobson writes: "When a nation is composed of millions of devoted, responsible family units, the entire society is stable, responsible and resilient." Do you agree or disagree? How does our society match up to this?

4. Keep in mind that fornication is defined as sexual intercourse on the part of unmarried persons. Then, using the following Bible references as resources, write a brief paragraph explaining the biblical view of premarital intercourse.

For from within, out of men's hearts, come evil thoughts, sexual immorality, theft, murder, adultery (Mark 7:21).

The body is not meant for sexual immorality, but for the Lord, and the Lord for the body. By his power God raised the Lord from the dead, and he will raise us also. Do you not know that your bodies are members of Christ himself? Shall I then take the members of Christ and unite them with a prostitute? Never! Do you not know that he who unites himself with a prostitute is one with her in body? For it is said, "The two will become one flesh." But he who unites himself with the Lord is one with him in spirit. Flee from sexual immorality. All other sins a man commits are outside his body, but he who sins sexually sins against his own body. Do you not know that your body is a temple of the Holy Spirit, who is in you, whom you have received from God? You are not your own; you were bought at a price. Therefore honor God with your body (1 Cor. 6:13-20).

The acts of the sinful nature are obvious: sexual immorality, impurity and debauchery; idolatry and witchcraft; hatred, discord, jealousy, fits of rage, selfish ambition, dissensions, factions and envy; drunkenness, orgies, and the like. I warn you, as I did before, that those who live like this will not inherit the kingdom of God (Gal. 5:19-21).

But everything exposed by the light becomes visible (Eph. 5:13).

Item 8: If a couple is genuinely in love, that condition is permanent—lasting a lifetime—true or false?

1. Dr. Dobson states: "Love, even genuine love, is a fragile thing. It must be maintained and protected if it is to survive." If you are married, identify and list three to five things you have experienced in your marriage that put a strain on your loving feelings. List three to five experiences that definitely strengthened your love for your spouse. (If you are engaged, or dating on a steady basis,

try talking together about this and identifying problems that could put a strain on a love relationship within marriage.)

2. Read 1 Corinthians 13:4-7 (see Item 1, Question 4, under Learning-Discussion Ideas) in as many versions as possible. From this Bible passage write a prescription for strengthening love.

3. Quickly go through your activities of the past few days. Based on what you did, decide where your marriage rates on your value scale. Is it getting scraps and leftovers from your busy schedule? Or are you treating your marriage as some thing of great worth? Make a "to do" list for the next three days. Take into account your work load, demands of your family, etc. Does your "to do" list include times with your spouse? Will you give these times number-one priority? Why? Why not?

Item 9: Short courtships (six months or less) are best—true or false?

1. To think through the validity of this statement, use the questions, statements and discussion ideas for Item 2.

2. Dr. Dobson believes that six months is far

too short a time for courtship. In your opinion, how long should a courtship last? How long did yours last? Could you have used more time to find out more about each other?

3. Is it possible for a courtship to be *too long*? Why?

4. If you are married, what did you learn about the personality and character of your mate after becoming husband and wife?

Item 10: Teenagers are more capable of genuine love than older people—true or false?

1. Genuine love demands caring for the other person, commitment to the other person, giving unselfishly of self. Why can these be difficult demands for teenagers to meet?

2. Compare Dr. Dobson's anniversary note to his wife with Ephesians 5:28-33. *In this same way, husbands ought to love their wives as their own bodies. He who loves his wife loves himself. After all, no one ever hated his own body, but he feeds and cares for it, just as Christ does the church—for we are members of his body. "For this reason a man will leave his father and mother and be united to his wife, and the two will become one flesh." This is a*

profound mystery—but I am talking about Christ and the church. However, each one of you also must love his wife as he loves himself, and the wife must respect her husband. What does the Ephesians Scripture passage have to say about being committed to one another? When you are committed to someone else, how do you feel? What do you say and do?

3. Read Genesis 2:24. *For this reason a man will leave his father and mother and be united to his wife, and they will become one flesh.* Discuss: What does it mean to become one flesh? List specific ways you and your spouse are one flesh.

CONCLUSION
Interpretation of Impressions

How can we know God's specific will for us in regard to the part romantic love will play in our lives? Have we been called to celibacy and singleness? If marriage is in the offing, how can we be sure we are listening to God in the choosing of a life's mate? How to determine God's will in that area of our lives may be the most important issue we, as Christians, ever confront, for therein lies the key to obedience—hence, to marital bliss.

Remember the example I gave in chapter four about the young man who was awakened by a dream in the middle of the night, a dream that convinced him he was called by God to marry a particular young lady? I also told you what a miserable marriage they had endured over the years. This marriage was based on an "interpretation of an impression," which turned out to be a terrible "mis"-interpretation.

Why? Wasn't that young man seeking the Lord's will in his life? Didn't that young lady want to be obedient to what she thought must be God's will for her? The answer to both of those questions is yes; but, unfortunately, the desire to serve and obey God must be guided by more than a vague impression.

It is true that God can and does speak directly to the heart. It is also true that it is the expressed purpose of the Holy Spirit to deal with human beings in a most personal and intimate way, convicting, directing and influencing. However, some people seem to find it very difficult to distinguish the voice of God from other sounds within.

We are told in 2 Corinthians 11:14 that the devil comes to us as "an angel of light," which means he counterfeits the work of the Holy Spirit. We must recognize that he has earned his reputation as the "father of lies" at the expense of those he has damned. There is no doubt in my mind that he often uses destructive impressions to implement his evil purposes. The Christian who accepts his own impressions at face value—uncritically—is extremely vulnerable to satanic mischief.

It is also important to remember that our

The human mind will often obediently convince itself of anything in order to have its own way.

impulses and thoughts are vulnerable to our physical condition and psychological situation at any given moment. Haven't you noticed that your impressions—as well as the love you may or may not "feel" toward your spouse, or how attractive or unattractive a member of the opposite sex may appear—are affected by the amount of sleep you had last night, and the state of your health, and your level of confidence at that time, and dozens of other forces that impinge upon your decision-making processes? We are trapped in these "earthen vessels," and our perception is necessarily influenced by our humanness.

In addition, our impressions may be interpreted by our "want to," which reminds me of the minister who received a call to a much larger and stronger church than he ever expected to lead. He replied, "I'll pray about it while my wife packs."

It is very difficult to separate the "want to" from our interpretation of God's will. The human mind will often obediently convince itself of anything in order to have its own way. Perhaps the most striking example of this self-delusion occurred with a young couple who decided to engage in sexual intercourse before marriage. Since the young man and woman were both reared in the church, they had to find a way to lessen the guilt from this forbidden act. So, they actually got down on their knees and prayed about what they

How can we know the purposes and leadings of the Lord for our lives regarding the issues of romantic love, and thus avoid destructive situations?

were going to do, and received "assurance" that it was all right to continue!

I am also acquainted with a family that was destroyed by an impression that could not have passed this very simple test: *Is it right?* Although there were four little children in the home, the mother felt she was "called" to leave them and enter full-time evangelistic work. On very short notice she abandoned the children who needed her so badly and left them in the care of their father who worked six and seven days a week.

The consequence was devastating. The youngest in the family lay awake at night, crying for his mommy. The older children had to assume adult responsibilities, which they were ill-prepared to carry. There was no one at home to train and love and guide the development of the lonely little family. I simply cannot believe the mother's impression was from God because it was neither scriptural nor "right" to leave the children. I suspect that she had other motives for fleeing her home, and Satan provided her with a seemingly noble explanation to cover her tracks.

How can we know, then, the purposes and leadings of the Lord for our lives regarding the issues of romantic love, and thus avoid such destructive situations as those mentioned above? In romantic love, as in any aspect of life, the key points to remember are:

- Many Christians depend exclusively on their impressions to determine the will of God.
- However, not all impressions are valid. Some are from God; some are from Satan; some are probably of our own making.
- Since it is difficult to determine the origin of an impression, we can easily make a mistake while assuming that a feeling is sent from God.
- Our Lord has promised to enlighten us and "guide us with his eye." On the other hand, He wants us to "test" our impressions and leadings.
- Therefore, every impression should be tested by four criteria before being accepted as valid:

1. Is it scriptural? This test involves more than taking a random proof text. It means studying what the whole Bible teaches. Use a concordance, search the Scriptures as did the Bereans (see Acts 17:11). Evaluate tentative leanings against the immutable Word of God.

2. Is it right? Every expression of God's will can be expected to conform to God's universal principles of morality and decency. If an impression would result in the depreciation of human worth or the integrity of the family or related traditional Christian values, it must be viewed with suspicion.

3. Is it providential? The third test requires every impression to be considered in the light of providential circumstances, such as: Are the necessary doors opening or closing? Do circumstances permit the implementation of what I feel to be God's will? Is the Lord speaking to me through events?

4. Is it reasonable? The final criterion against which the will of God is measured relates to the appropriateness of the act. Does it make sense? Is it consistent with the character of God to require it? Will this act contribute to the Kingdom?

- Satan will offer false representatives of the will of God, including astrologers, witches, mediums, false teachers, etc. We must scrupulously avoid these alternatives and "hold fast to that which is good."
- There will be times when the will of God will not be abundantly clear to us. During those occasions we are expected to retain our faith and "wait on the Lord."

Ultimately, the comprehension of God's will requires a careful balance between rational deliberation on one hand, and emotional responses on the other. Each Christian must find that balance in his own relationship with God, yielding to the teachings of the Holy Spirit.

A PERSONAL POSTSCRIPT

During a Marriage Encounter weekend in 1981, I wrote a letter to my wife, Shirley. Following is a portion of that letter (minus some introductory intimacies), which, I believe, sums up the depth and intensity of the kind of rich, romantic love that can be experienced only by two individuals who share a lifelong commitment to God and to each other.

Who else shares the memory of my youth during which the foundations of love were laid?

I ask you, who else could occupy the place that is reserved for the only woman who was *there* when I graduated from college and went to the Army and returned as a student at USC and bought my first decent car (and promptly wrecked it) and picked out an inexpensive wedding ring with you (and paid for it with Savings Bonds) and we prayed and thanked God for what we had. Then we said the wedding vows and my dad prayed, "Lord, you gave us Jimmy and Shirley as infants to love and cherish and raise for a season, and tonight, we give them back to you after our labor of love—not as two separate individuals, but as one!" And everyone cried.

Then we left for the honeymoon and spent all our money and came home to an apartment full of rice and a bell on the bed, and we had only just begun. You taught the second grade and I taught (and fell in love with) a bunch of sixth graders and especially a kid named Norbert and I earned a master's degree and passed the comprehensive exams for a doctorate and we bought our first little home and remodeled it and I dug up all the grass and buried it in a 10-foot hole which later sank and looked like two graves in the front yard—and while spreading the dirt to make a new lawn, I accidentally "planted" eight million ash seeds from our tree and discovered two weeks later that we had a forest growing between our house and the street.

Then, alas, you delivered our very own baby and we loved her half to death and named her Danae Ann and built a room on our little bungalow and gradually filled it with furniture. Then I joined the staff at Children's Hospital and I did well there, but still didn't have enough money to pay our USC tuition and other expenses so we sold (and ate) a Volkswagen. Then I earned a Ph.D. and we cried and thanked God for what we had.

In 1970, we brought home a little boy and named him James Ryan and loved him half to death and didn't sleep for six months. And I labored over a manuscript titled "Dare To" something or other and then reeled backward under a flood of favorable responses and a few not-so-favorable responses and received a small royalty check and thought it was a fortune and I joined the faculty at USC School of Medicine and did well there.

Soon I found myself pacing the halls of Huntington Memorial Hospital as a team of grim-faced neurologists examined your nervous system for evidence of hypothalamic tumor and I prayed and begged God to let me complete my life with my best friend, and He finally said, "Yes—for now," and we cried and thanked Him for what we had.

And we bought a new house and promptly tore it to shreds and went skiing in Vail, Colorado, and tore your leg to shreds and I called your mom to report the accident and she tore me to shreds and our toddler, Ryan, tore the whole town of Arcadia to shreds. And the construction on the house seemed to go on forever and you stood in the shattered living room and cried every Saturday night because so little had been accomplished. Then during the worst of the mess, 100 friends gave us a surprise housewarming and they slopped through the debris and mud and sawdust and cereal bowls and sandwich parts—and the next morning you groaned and asked, "Did it really happen?"

And I published a new book called *Hide or Seek* (What?) and everyone called it *Hide* and *Seek* and the publisher sent us to Hawaii and we stood on the balcony overlooking the bay and thanked God for what we had. And I published *What Wives Wish* and people liked it and the honors rolled in and the speaking requests arrived by the hundreds. Then you underwent risky surgery and I said, "Lord, not now!" And the doctor said, "No cancer!" and we cried and thanked God for what we had.

Then I started a radio program and took a leave of absence from Children's Hospital and opened a little office in Arcadia called Focus on the Family, which a 3-year-old radio listener later called "Poke us in the Family," and we got more visible. Then we went to Kansas City for a family vacation and my dad prayed on the last day and said, "Lord, we know it can't always be the wonderful way it is now, but we thank you for the love we enjoy today." A month later he experienced his heart attack and in December I said goodbye to my gentle friend and you put your arm around me and said, "I'm hurting with you!" and I cried and said, "I love you!"

And we invited my mother to spend six weeks with us during her recuperation period and the three of us endured the loneliest Christmas of our lives as the empty chair and missing place setting reminded us of his red sweater and dominoes and apples and a stack of sophisticated books and a little dog named Benji who always sat on his lap.

But life went on. My mother staggered to get herself back together and couldn't and lost 15 pounds and moved to California and still ached for her missing friend. And more books were written and more honors arrived and we became better known and our influence spread and we thanked God for what we had.

And our daughter went into adolescence and this great authority on children knew he was inadequate and found himself asking God to help him with the awesome task of parenting and He did and we thanked Him for sharing His wisdom with us. And then a little dog named Siggie who was sort of a dachshund grew old and toothless and we had to let the vet do his thing, and a 15-year love affair between man and dog ended with a whimper. But a pup named Mindy showed up at the front door and life went on.

Then a series of films was produced in San Antonio, Texas, and our world turned upside down as we were thrust into the fishbowl and "Poke us in the Family" expanded in new directions and life got busier and more hectic and time became more precious and then someone invited us to a Marriage Encounter weekend where I sit at this moment.

So I ask you! Who's gonna take your place in my life? You have become me and I have become you. We are inseparable. I've now spent 46 percent of my life with you, and I can't even remember much of the first 54! Not one of the experiences I've listed can be comprehended by anyone but the woman who lived through them with me. Those days are gone, but their aroma lingers on in our minds. And with every event during these 21 years, our lives have become more intertwined—blending eventually into this incredible affection that I bear for you today.

Is it any wonder that I can read your face like a book when we are in a crowd? The slightest narrowing of your eyes speaks volumes to me about the thoughts that are running through your conscious experience. As you open Christmas presents, I know instantly if you like the color or style of the gift, because your feelings cannot be hidden from me.

I love you, S.M.D. (Remember the monogrammed shirt?) I love the girl who believed in me before I believed in myself. I love the girl who never complained about huge school bills and books and hot apartments and rented junky furniture and no vacations and humble little Volkswagens. You have been *with* me—encouraging me, loving me and supporting me since August 27, 1960. And the status you have given me in our home is beyond what I have deserved.

So why do I want to go on living? It's because I have you to take that journey with. Otherwise, why make the trip? The half life that lies ahead promises to be tougher than the years behind us. It is in the nature of things that my mom will someday join my father and then she will be laid to rest beside him in Olathe, Kansas, overlooking a windswept hill from whence he walked with Benji and recorded a cassette tape for me describing the beauty of that spot. Then we'll have to say goodbye to your mom and dad. Gone will be the table games we played and the Ping-Pong and lawn darts and Joe's laughter and Alma's wonderful ham dinners and her underlined birthday cards and the little yellow house in Long Beach. Everything within me screams "No!" But my dad's final prayer is still valid—"We know it can't always be the way it is now." When that time comes, our childhoods will then be severed—cut off by the passing of the beloved parents who bore us.

What then, my sweet wife? To whom will I turn for solace and comfort? To whom can I say,

"I'm hurting!" and know that I am understood in more than an abstract manner? To whom can I turn when the summer leaves begin to change colors and fall to the ground? How much I have enjoyed the springtime and the warmth of the summer sun. The flowers and the green grass and the blue sky and the clear streams have been savored to their fullest.

But, alas, autumn is coming. Even now, I can feel a little nip in the air—and I try not to look at a distant, lone cloud that passes near the horizon. I must face the fact that winter lies ahead—with its ice and sleet and snow to pierce us through. But in this instance, winter will not be followed by springtime, except in the glory of the life to come. With whom, then, will I spend that final season of my life?

None but you, Shirls. The only joy of the future will be in experiencing it as we have the past 21 years—hand in hand with the one I love . . . a young miss named Shirley Deere, who gave me everything she had—including her heart.

Thank you, babe, for making this journey with me. Let's finish it—together!

Your Jim*

*From *Love Must Be Tough* by James Dobson (Dallas: Word Books, 1986). Used by permission.

ABOUT THE AUTHOR

♡

James C. Dobson, Ph.D. is founder and president of Focus on the Family, a non-profit organization that produces his nationally syndicated radio program, heard daily on more than 1,300 stations. He was for 14 years an Associate Clinical Professor of Pediatrics at the University of Southern California School of Medicine and served for 17 years on the Attending Staff of Children's Hospital of Los Angeles in the Divisions of Child Development and Medical Genetics. He is the author of many best-selling books for the family, including **Parenting Isn't for Cowards, Hide or Seek, Love for a Lifetime,** and **The Strong-Willed Child.** Dr. Dobson served on the Task Force which summarized the White House Conferences on the Family, and received a special commendation from President Jimmy Carter in 1980. He was also appointed by President Reagan to the National Advisory Committee for Juvenile Justice and Delinquency Prevention, 1982-86, and to the Attorney General's Committee on Pornography. Dr. Dobson and his wife Shirley have two grown children and live in Southern California.

Other Materials
For the Family
by
Dr. James Dobson

Regal Books

Emotions: Can You Trust Them? Dr. Dobson explores the important emotions which play powerful roles in our lives. 5418350 ISBN 0-8307-0996-7

Preparing for Adolescence Dr. Dobson talks directly with pre-teens about issues facing them, inferiority, puberty, love and identity. 5419314
ISBN 0-8307-1258-5

Preparing for Adolescence Leader's Guide New, revised Leader's Guide correlates to new *Preparing for Adolescence*. Available, 12/89. V0689

Preparing for Adolescence Parent Guide All-new book designed to help families use the new *Preparing for Adolescence*. Available, 6/90. 5203067 ISBN 0-8307-1389-1

Listen and Grow Cassette Tapes

Preparing for Adolescence This eight-cassette album is designed to help parents and pre-teenagers prepare for the changes they are facing. A127760

Discipline from Cradle to College This six-cassette album is based on the positive, constructive concepts discussed in *Dare to Discipline* and *The Strong-Willed Child*. A287627

Kids Need Self-Esteem Too This six-cassette album presents ways parents and teachers can strengthen self-confidence and self-worth in children. A287782

What Wives Wish Their Husbands Knew About Women In this six-cassette album, Dr. Dobson identifies the most common causes of depression in women and offers specific steps toward recovery and peace. A287555

Buy these books and cassette albums from your regular Christian supplier.

OTHER MATERIALS
BY DR. JAMES DOBSON

Dare to Discipline, Tyndale, 1970.

Hide or Seek: How to Build Self-Esteem in Your Child, Revell, 1974.

What Wives Wish Their Husbands Knew About Women, Tyndale, 1975.

The Strong-Willed Child, Tyndale, 1978.

Straight Talk to Men and Their Wives, Word, 1980.

Emotions: Can You Trust Them?, Regal Books, 1980.

Dr. Dobson Answers Your Questions, Tyndale, 1982.

Love Must Be Tough, Word, 1983.

Love for a Lifetime, Multnomah Press, 1987.

Parenting Isn't for Cowards, Word, 1987.

These and other items are available in local bookstores or may be ordered by writing Focus on the Family, Pomona, California 91799. Dr. Dobson also may be contacted through that address.